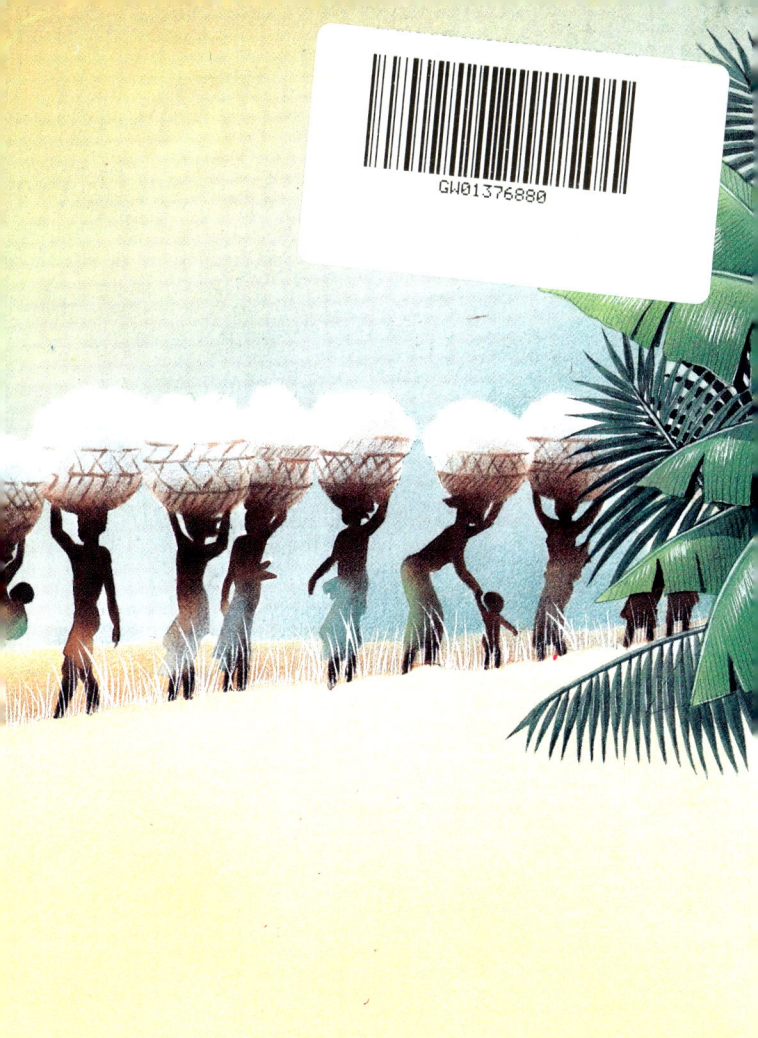

Written and illustrated by Aline Riquier

*Specialist adviser:
Cotton Council International*

*ISBN 1 85103 179 0
First published 1993 in the United Kingdom
by Moonlight Publishing Ltd,
36 Stratford Road, London W8
Translated by Sarah Matthews*

© 1991 by Editions Gallimard
English text © 1993 by Moonlight Publishing Ltd
Printed in Italy by Editoriale Libraria

POCKET ● WORLDS

Cotton
from Seed to Cloth

It grows on a bush,
we've been using it for 7,000 years,
it keeps us warm in cold weather
and cool when it's hot...

THE WORLD WE USE

In the mountains, a cotton tent gives good shelter.

On the Nile, the feluccas have cotton sails.

In China, people wear jackets padded with cotton.

In the desert, cotton robes give protection from sun and wind.

If you cut yourself, what do you wipe the wound with? Cotton. Every day you put on underwear; what is it made of? Cotton.

People the world over wear clothes made of cotton.

Cotton is light and cool
for hot countries; when
padded, it is soft and warm
for cold countries.
It can be made into sails,
tents, curtains, umbrellas, blinds...

Cotton clothes are soft and comfortable to wear. If you sweat, the cotton soaks up the moisture like blotting paper, and when cotton fibres are wet they become tougher than ever. You can wash cotton again and again in very hot water. You can disinfect it with special chemicals to kill any germs: cotton is very useful in hospitals.

Some cotton flowers are yellow; others are pink and turn red.

Where does cotton come from?

Cotton grows on plants.
In the wild, cotton plants can
grow up to seven metres high
and live for at least ten years.
Cultivated cotton plants are much smaller
and only live for a year.

Cotton seeds

Two months after planting, the branches
of the little bush are covered in flowers.
They are so lovely that the Chinese used
to use them to decorate their houses.

The ripe pods split open to let out the cotton bolls inside.

After three days, the flowers fade and drop.
In their place are small green fruits,
the pods. Inside the pods, the seeds are
wrapped round with soft white fibres:
these are fibres of cotton!

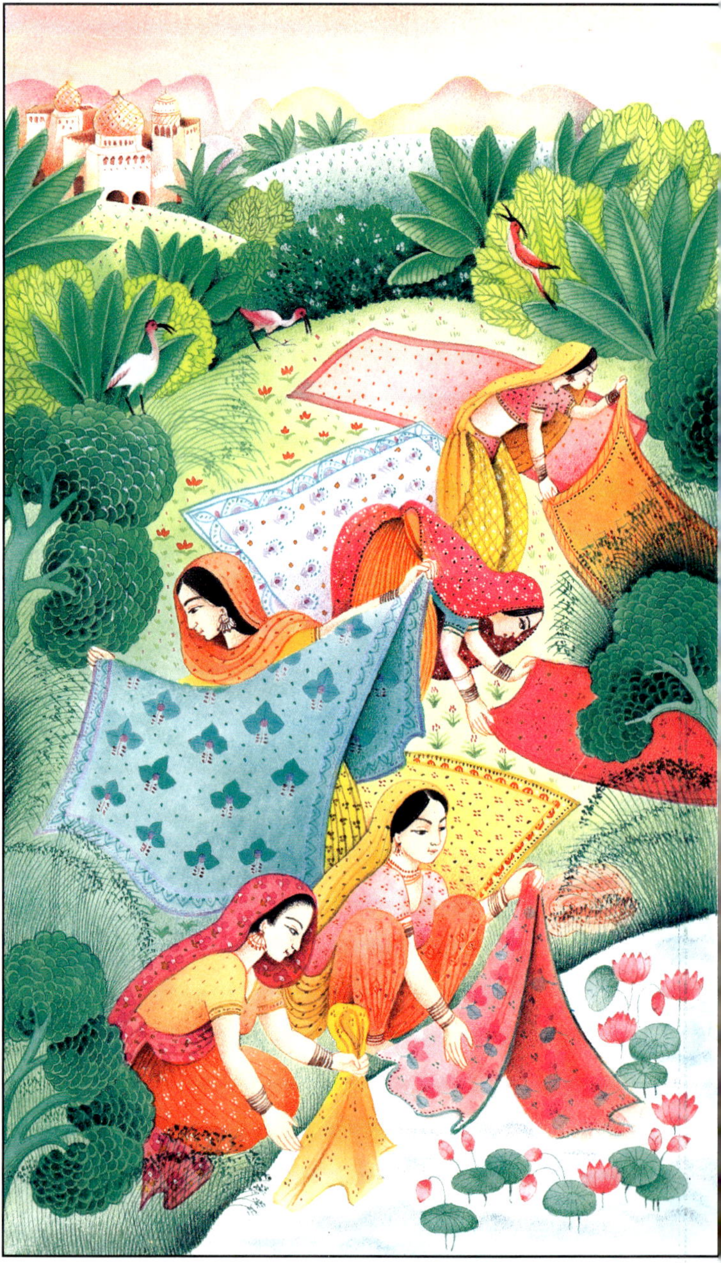

From east to west, cotton plants span the globe.

In Asia and in America, people have been growing and weaving cotton for at least 7,000 years! Archaeologists have found traces of cotton and of cotton cloth in tombs in Mexico and Pakistan.
In the valley of the Indus, in Pakistan, skill in cotton growing and weaving made the people rich. They had even invented machines to separate the seeds from the fibres.

How did cotton get to Europe?

It was brought by the Arabs in the ninth century. The Arab word, kutun or ketan, gave us the name we use today: cotton!

Tapestry from Peru

In the sixteenth century, cotton clothes were expensive and only the rich could afford them. But then English and Dutch traders began to ship huge quantities of cotton from America. Cotton clothing soon became cheap and popular.

Cotton was grown on large plantations in the southern United States. Picking cotton by hand, one boll at a time, was slow, back-breaking work. The planters brought in slaves from Africa to do this job. Now cotton is harvested by huge machines which pull the cotton fibres from the plants.

Today, we all wear clothes made of cotton. Cotton plants grow wherever the weather is hot and there is plenty of water. Over seventy countries grow cotton. The biggest producers in the world are China, America and the states of the former USSR.

In Europe, cotton is only grown in Greece
and Spain, but Europeans are skilled
at processing and weaving the cotton
imported from Africa, America and Asia.
Cotton production provides millions
of people all over the world with work
and an income to live on.

16

How does cotton grow?

When the weather is damp and rainy, the seeds are sown in straight rows in the soil that has been prepared for them. A week afterwards, the first seedlings start to appear. The young plants need lots of sunshine and lots of water. They also need protection from pests and weeds.

Greenfly, caterpillars and spiders can all harm the leaves and pods.

In the big plantations of America, most of the work is carried out using huge machines. In Africa, though, much of the work is still done by hand.

This aeroplane is flying low over the plants, dusting them with chemicals to kill the pests.

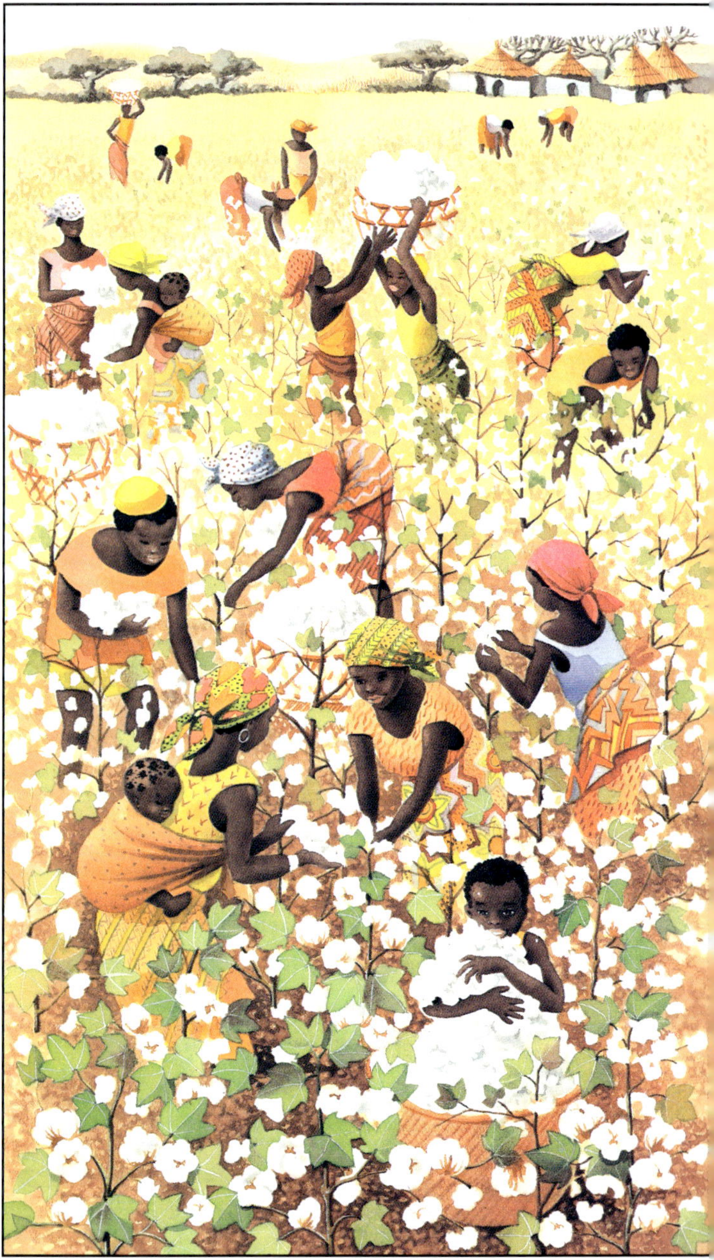

In the fields, the pods ripen and split.

They are ready to be harvested. The whole village joins in. The ripe pods are picked carefully, while others are left to ripen a little more, to be picked another day. When the pods are harvested by machine, all the pods are picked at the same time, along with some leaves and twigs as well! They will have to be sorted out afterwards. One machine can do the same amount of work as one hundred people. Trucks take the cotton to the cotton gins, where the fibres are separated from the seeds.

Machines tip the pods into huge trucks.

In America, the cotton from one batch is baled in the fields.

As evening falls over the African plains, the villagers come in from the fields to their round mud houses, each carrying a huge basket laden with its precious burden of cotton.

The baskets are emptied out onto the flat ground in the centre of the village, until it looks as if it is covered in drifting snow! Then, under the watchful gaze of the monkeys in the trees, the cotton is weighed and sold.

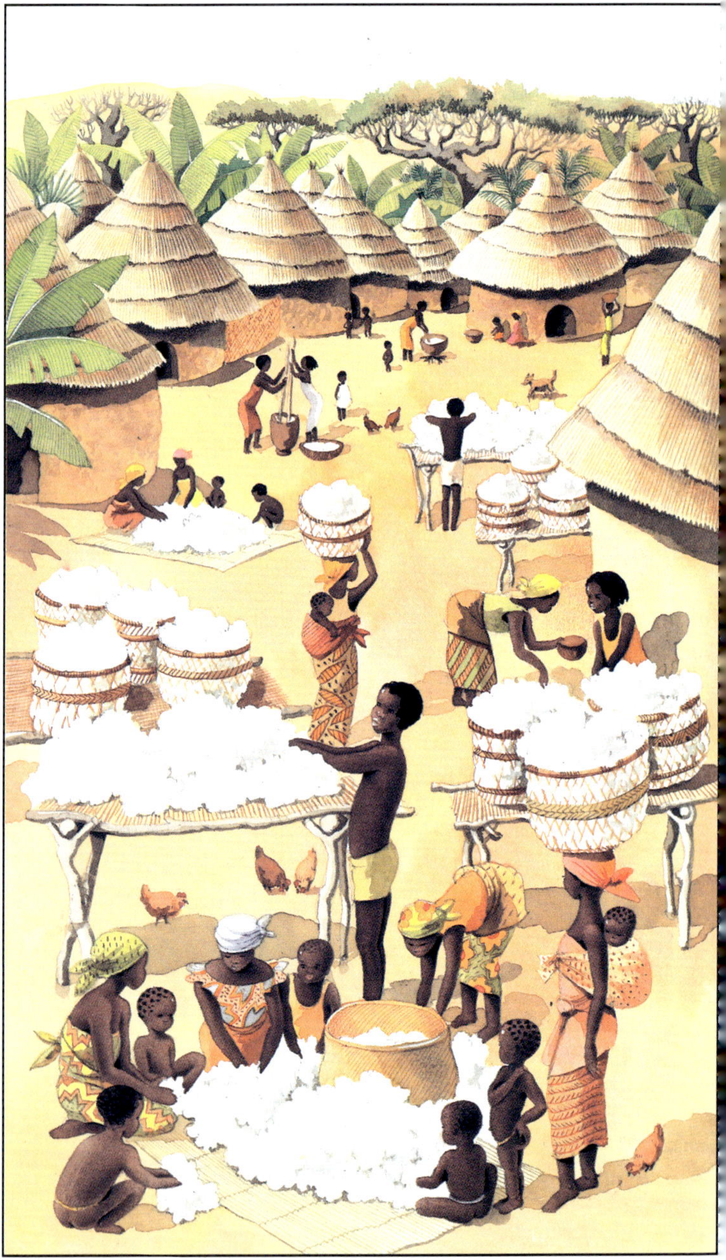

A pod    **A seed surrounded by fibres**   **The seeds and fibres are separated.**

What is there inside a cotton pod?

Each pod contains two separate crops: cotton seeds and cotton fibres. Each seed is surrounded by tiny threads, about as long as your finger. These are the cotton fibres.

The longer and whiter the fibres are, the better the quality of the cotton.

So that it can be carried easily, the cotton is pressed into huge bales tied together with iron hoops.

What happens to the cotton seed?

Some is kept to plant for next year's crop, but most is crushed to make oil which can be used for cooking. The seed kernels are used for cattle-feed and fertilizer.

The bales of cotton are shipped to the cotton mills.

From fibre to yarn

Thread by thread, the fibres are teased out and twisted together. The yarn is spun round a stick called a spindle.

Spindle and spinning wheel

From yarn to cloth

People have been weaving yarn into cloth for many thousands of years.

The yarn is stretched over a wooden frame.

Yarn is stretched, a thread at a time, across the loom. Then other threads are woven in and out across them with a shuttle.

Navajo Indians weave cotton cloth in colourful patterns.

Even today, high in the Andes, Peruvians weave ponchos and blankets in multi-coloured patterns on hand looms.

A loom from the Persian Gulf

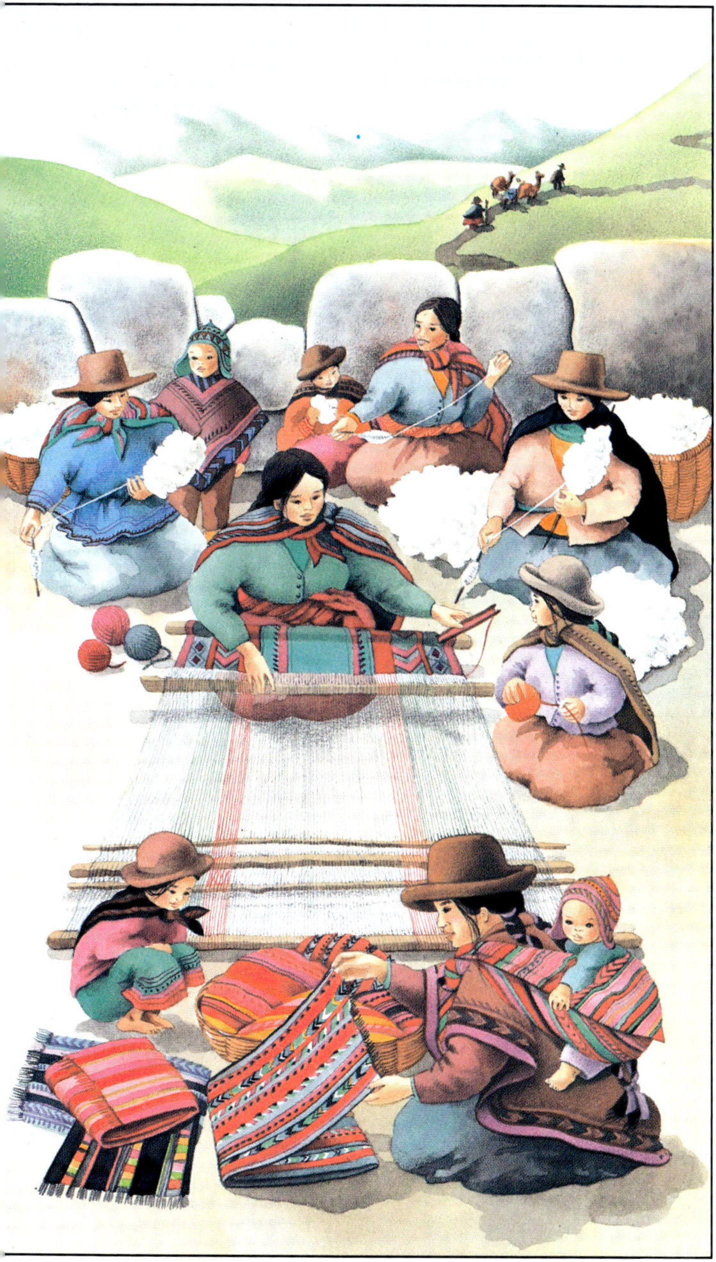

1. The bales are cleaned and sorted.

2. The cleaned cotton is combed and pulled into long webs.

Most cotton these days is processed by huge machines. There are machines to clean the cotton, to sort it, to comb it, and to spin it into yarn. The more the yarn is twisted as it is spun, the stronger it becomes.

The fabric woven from raw cotton is a pale golden colour. It has to be bleached and washed to make it white.

5. The thread is wound onto bobbins and cylinders.

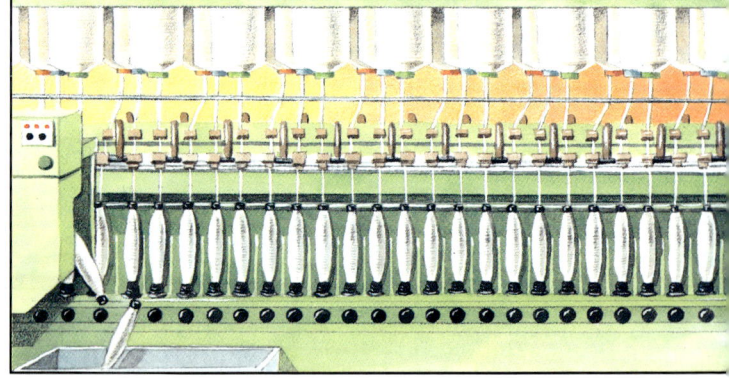

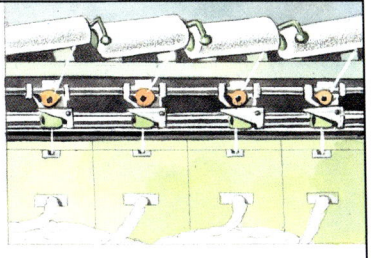

3. Several webs are drawn together into a rope, or sliver.

4. The slivers are pulled out and twisted into yarn.

The fabric can be treated so it does not crease or shrink – it can even be treated to make it waterproof!

Cotton mix fabrics

In the twentieth century, cotton yarn is sometimes mixed with other, man-made, synthetic fibres, made from wood, coal, or even petrol.

6. On shuttleless looms, the yarn is sent across the threads by a jet of air.

7. A cylinder knitting machine produces a tube of cloth.

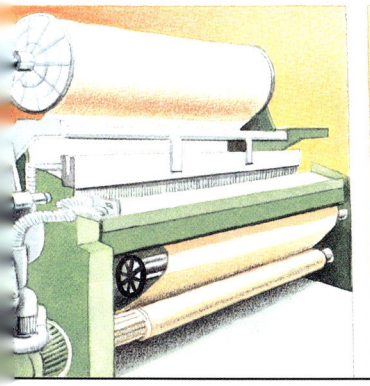

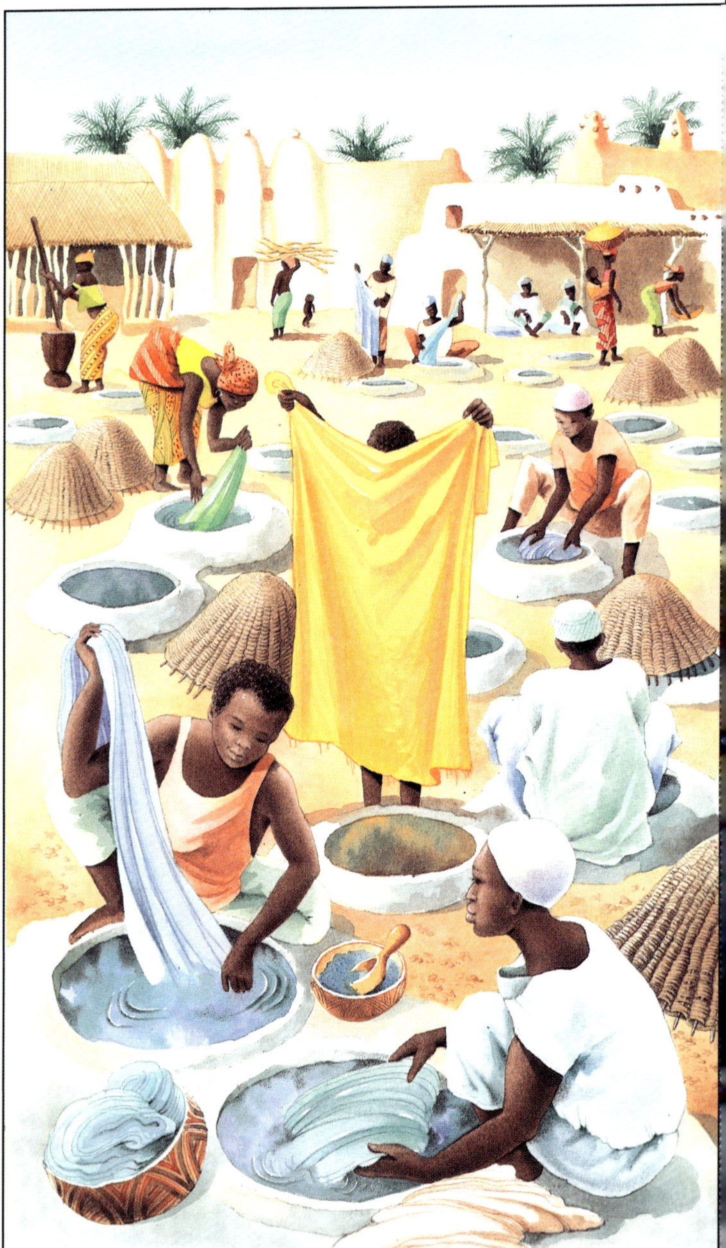

Multi-coloured cloth!

For thousands of years, people have dyed cloths with colours made from plants: indigo blue, madder red, saffron yellow. Now, chemical dyes are often used, though people are rediscovering vegetable dyes.

The yarn is dipped into the dye.

The cloth is knotted before being dyed.

Brush and stamp

How can patterns be printed onto cloth?

You need brushes, pads, paintbrushes, rollers... Sometimes patterns are painted on in wax, so that they stay white when the cloth is dyed. Sometimes screens are used, so that large areas of cloth can be printed at once. Roller print machines can print lengths of cloth with up to twenty colours, one after the other.

A printing roller

Velvet Jersey Canvas

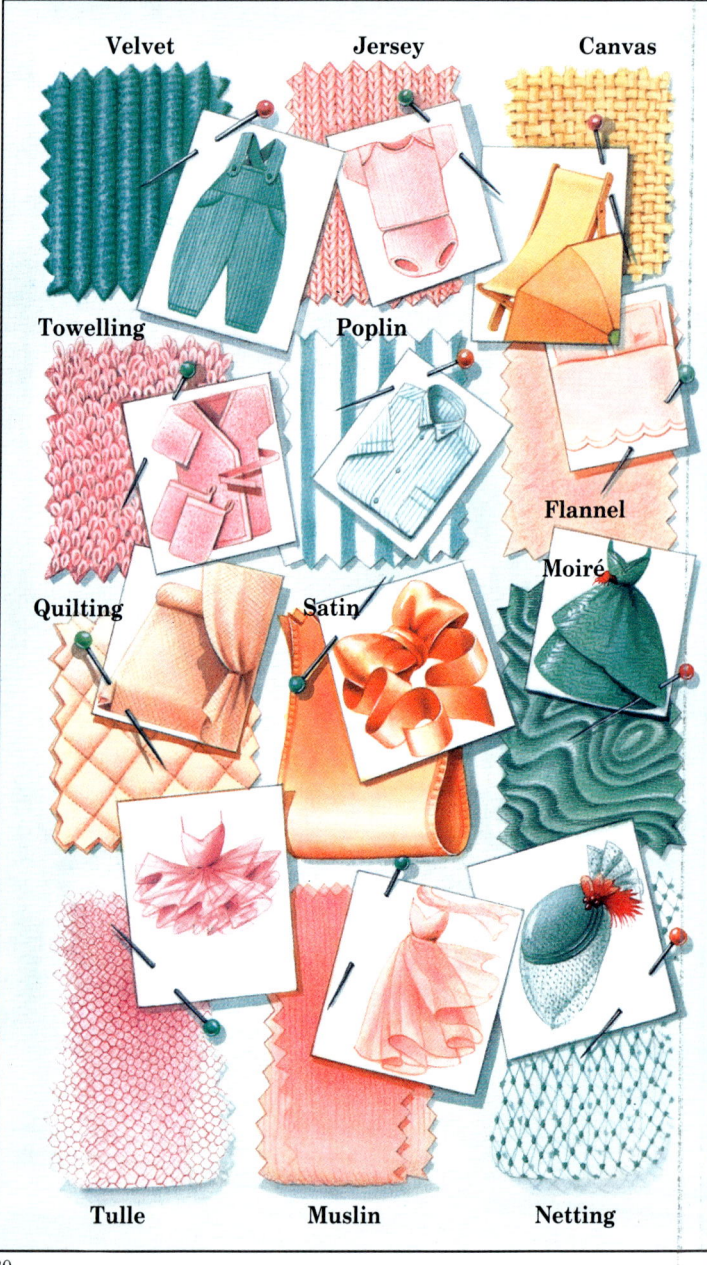

Towelling Poplin

Flannel

Quilting Satin

Moiré

Tulle Muslin Netting

There are so many different kinds of cloth!

Some cloths, such as poplin, are as smooth as can be, some like muslin are light enough to float away, some make lovely party clothes, like tulle or moiré, some are tough like denim for jeans, some are soft and absorbent, like towelling...

Crocheted, knitted, knotted or made into the finest lace – cotton can be made to do almost anything you can imagine!
Do you know how to embroider?
Lovely patterns can be sewn with coloured threads, using different stitches to create interesting textures.

Other plant fibres can be used to make cloth as well.

Linen fibres are widely used the world over. Ancient Egyptians used to wear clothes made of woven linen.

Hemp has a very thick, tough fibre, which is excellent for making sacks and ropes.

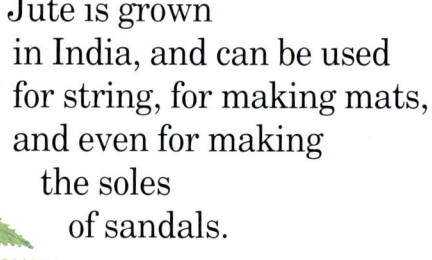

Jute is grown in India, and can be used for string, for making mats, and even for making the soles of sandals.

Ramie is a plant from the same family as flax, and the cloth made from its fibres looks rather like linen. It is grown in the Far East.

Sisal comes from the agave plant, which grows well in hot countries, and particularly in Mexico. It is good for making ropes and hammocks, or hard-wearing carpets.

One small animal makes an extremely precious thread: silk. Silk is made by silkworms, which are the larvae of a butterfly. The larvae weave cocoons of the finest, shiniest threads, which, when unravelled and woven, make some of the most beautiful cloth in the world.

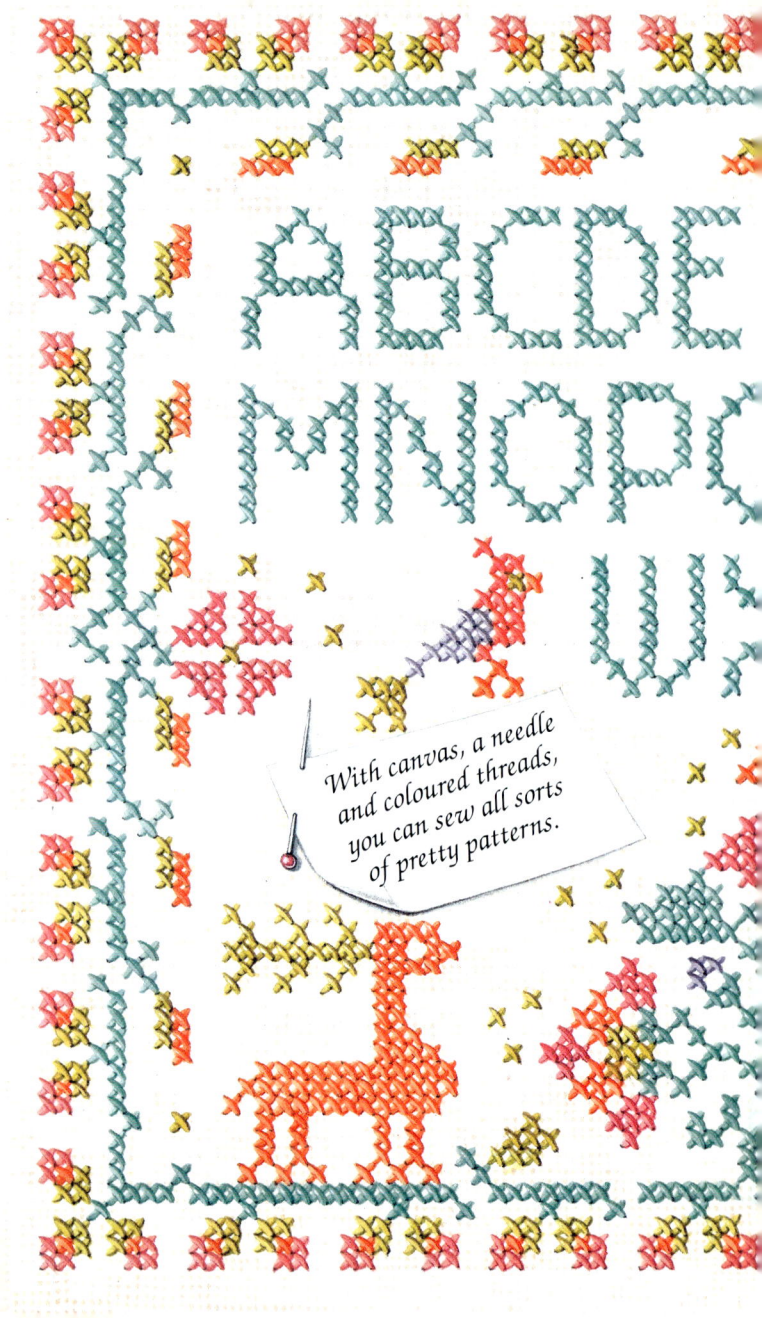

With canvas, a needle and coloured threads, you can sew all sorts of pretty patterns.

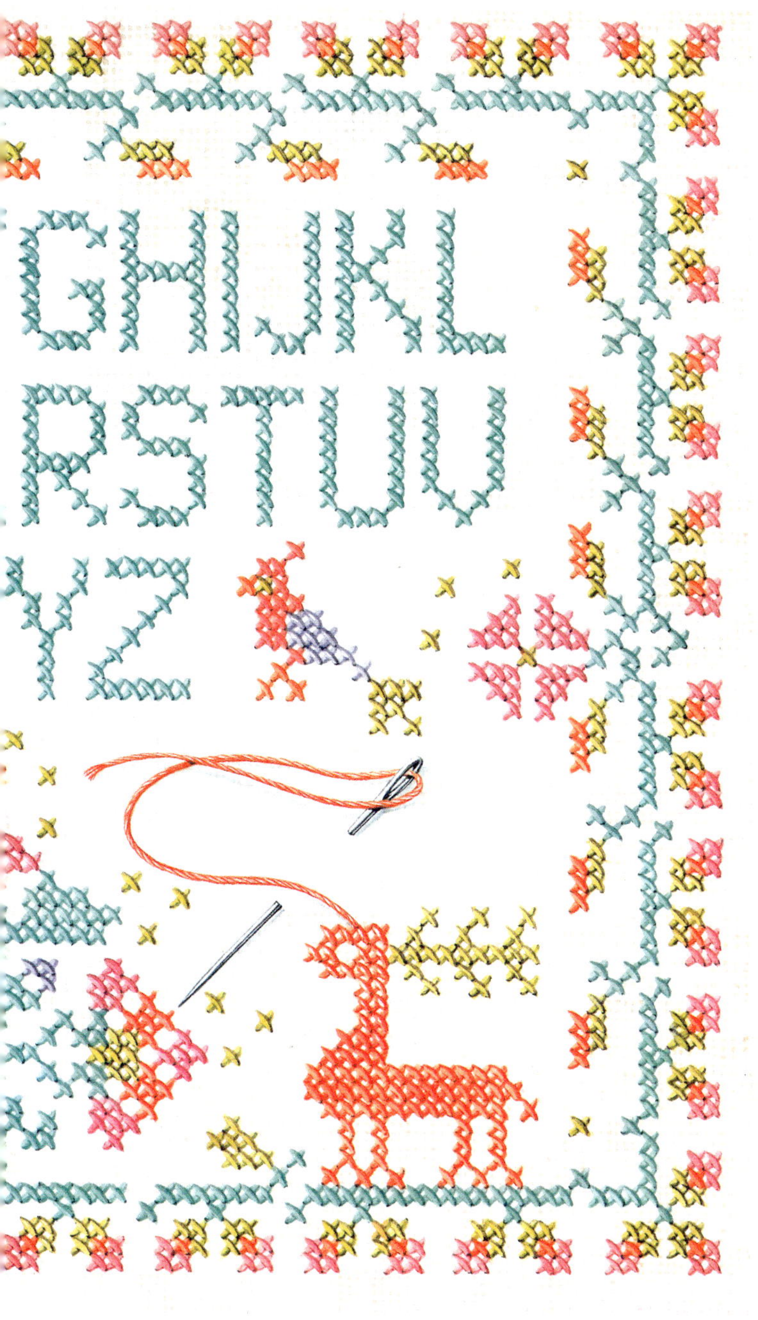
GHIJKL
RSTUV
YZ

Index

Africa, 15, 17, 20
America, 11, 13, 14, 17
Asia, 11
bale, 23, 26
bobbin, 26
boll, 9
China, 6, 14
cloth, 24
cotton flower, 8, 9
cotton plants, 9-23
cotton products, 6-7
cotton-mix fabrics, 27
dyeing, 29
embroidery, 31, 34
Europe, 11-12
fibres, 9, 11, 19, 23-4

flowers, 8-9
gin, 19
growing, 17
harvesting, 19-21
hemp, 32
jute, 32
linen, 32
padded cotton, 6, 7
Peru, 24
pests, 17
plantations, 13-17
pods, 19, 23
printing, 29
ramie, 33
seed, 9, 11, 19, 23
seed oil, 23

shuttle, 24
silk, 33
sisal, 33
spindle, 24
spinning, 26
synthetic fibres, 27
treating cotton, 27
types of cloth, 30-31
USSR, 14
weaving, 24-7
web, 26-7
yarn, 24-7

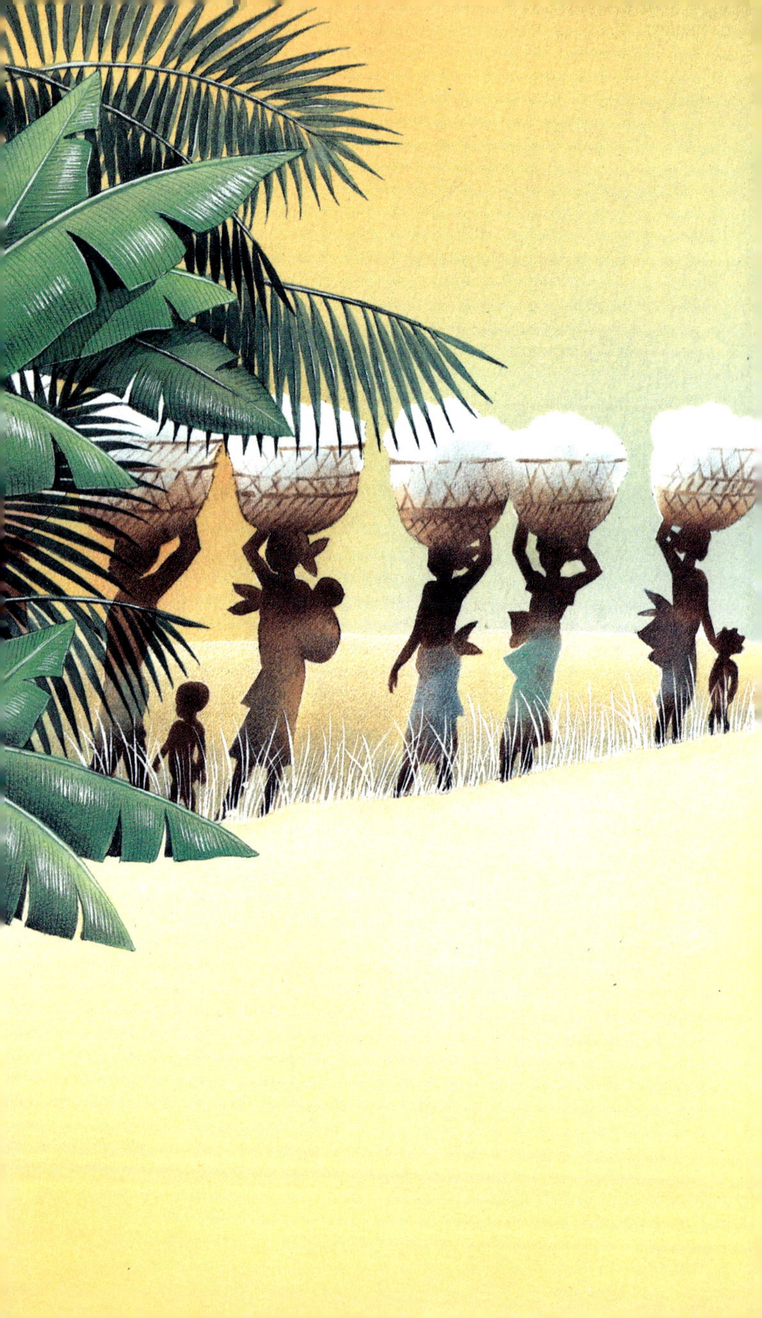